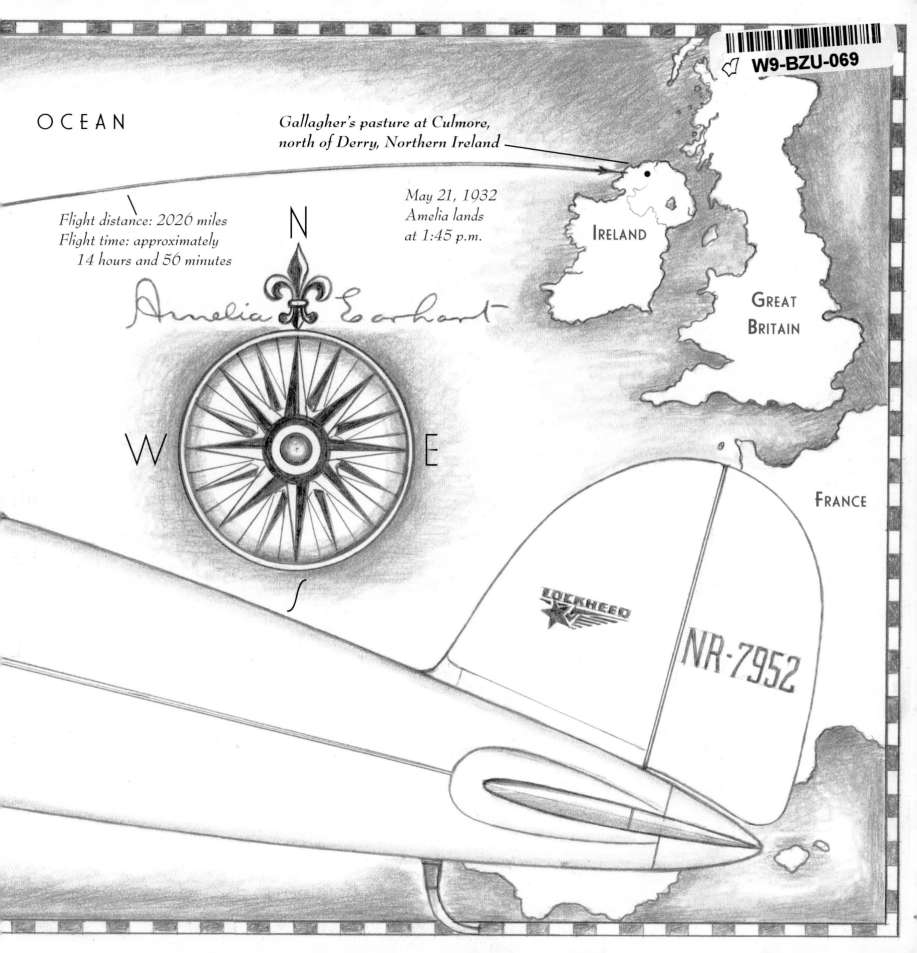

OCEAN

Gallagher's pasture at Culmore,
north of Derry, Northern Ireland

IRELAND

GREAT
BRITAIN

May 21, 1932
Amelia lands
at 1:45 p.m.

Flight distance: 2026 miles
Flight time: approximately
14 hours and 56 minutes

Amelia Earhart

N

W   E

S

FRANCE

LOCKHEED

NR-7952

"To all my friends, both near and far,
let me say that you will hear from me
in less than fifteen hours."

Amelia Earhart

A Paula Wiseman Book
· Simon & Schuster Books for Young Readers ·
New York   London   Toronto   Sydney

Night Flight

AMELIA EARHART
CROSSES THE ATLANTIC

ROBERT BURLEIGH

PAINTINGS BY WENDELL MINOR

ACKNOWLEDGMENTS

I would like to acknowledge the many people who aided me in my research for this book. A special thanks to astronaut Eileen Collins for her meaningful introduction to *Night Flight*. She has carried on in the spirit of Amelia Earhart. Many thanks also to Dorothy Cochrane, curator in the Aeronautics Department of the Smithsonian National Air and Space Museum, for her guidance on the details of Amelia's Lockheed Vega in their collection in Washington; to Keith Ferris, America's premier aviation artist, for sharing his expertise and schematic drawings of the original Vega design; and to Kermit Weeks at Fantasy of Flight for allowing my photographer, Tom Reid, to photograph the Lockheed Vega in his collection. I am also grateful for the use of the George Palmer Putnam collection of Amelia Earhart's archives at Purdue University.

—W. M.

SIMON & SCHUSTER BOOKS FOR YOUNG READERS • An imprint of Simon & Schuster Children's Publishing Division • 1230 Avenue of the Americas, New York, New York 10020 • Text copyright © 2011 by Robert Burleigh • Illustrations copyright © 2011 by Wendell Minor • All rights reserved, including the right of reproduction in whole or in part in any form. • SIMON & SCHUSTER BOOKS FOR YOUNG READERS is a trademark of Simon & Schuster, Inc. • For information about special discounts for bulk purchases, please contact Simon & Schuster Special Sales at 1-866-506-1949 or business@simonandschuster.com. • The Simon & Schuster Speakers Bureau can bring authors to your live event. For more information or to book an event, contact the Simon & Schuster Speakers Bureau at 1-866-248-3049 or visit our website at www.simonspeakers.com. • Book design by Laurent Linn • The text for this book is set in Bernhard Modern. • The illustrations for this book are rendered in gouache and watercolor on Strathmore 500 3-ply bristol board. • Manufactured in China • 0511 SCP • 10 9 8 7 6 5 4 3 2 • Library of Congress Cataloging-in-Publication Data • Burleigh, Robert. • Night flight : Amelia Earhart crosses the Atlantic / Robert Burleigh ; illustrated by Wendell Minor. • p. cm. • "A Paula Wiseman Book." • Summary: An account of Amelia Earhart's dangerous 1932 flight across the Atlantic Ocean from Newfoundland to Ireland, in which she survived bad weather and a malfunctioning airplane. Includes a brief biography of the aviator. • Includes bibliographical references. • ISBN 978-1-4169-6733-0 (hardcover) • 1. Earhart, Amelia, 1897–1937—Voyages and travels—Juvenile literature. 2. Air pilots—United States—Biography—Juvenile literature. 3. Transatlantic flights—Juvenile literature. [1. Earhart, Amelia, 1897–1937. 2. Air pilots. 3. Transatlantic flights.] I. Minor, Wendell, ill. • II. Title. • TL540.E3B874 2011   629.1309163'1-dc22   2008052269

For Lulu Freeland—up, up, and away!

—R. B.

To astronaut Eileen Collins, NASA's first female shuttle pilot and commander,
and in memory of my friend and pilot Linda Head Neumann.

—W. M.

From high in the cockpit, a woman gazes down.
It is exactly 7:12 p.m.

The sunset ripples over the rough-hewn airfield.
Good-bye, my friends, good-bye!

Amelia Earhart pushes her last doubts into a secret place deep inside her.
It is here: the hour, the very minute. Go!

The red Vega rolls down the runway.
Faster, then faster.

The plane swoops like a swallow
over dark puddles and patches of tundra.

The shore gleams in the waning light.
The waves are curls of cream-colored froth.

The plane ascends, high and higher,
as the pounding surf turns noiseless below.

Amelia Earhart lives for this moment:
to follow the wide horizon that never ends!

The moon peeks between wisps of shimmering clouds.
Distant stars flicker and fade. Her mind soars.

She loves what she likes to call "first-time things."
She remembers roller coasters, bicycles, barebacked horses.

She sees herself standing again, a young girl, before whirling propellers.
The props send puffs of soft snow into her delighted eyes.

What she has seen from above! Mountains like wrinkles in the earth,
cities like toy blocks, cars like ants, and the blue Pacific glittering into mist.

And now—she must cross this dark and seething ocean.
Why? Because "women must try to do things as men have tried."

The gentle night nestles around her on every side.
She rides easy, soothed by the engine's constant drone.

She thinks this journey will be like so many others: simple, soon over.
But she is wrong.

Midnight.
The blackness erupts. Clouds heave. The sky unlocks.

Fists of rain pummel the cockpit windshield.
Rivers of quicksilver darkness drown the moon.

The wooden Vega wobbles on invisible hills of air.
Lightning scribbles its zigzag warning across the sky: DANGER.

Amelia Earhart wakes from her half dream. Is it thunder?
Or her heart pounding in brief, sudden spurts?

She shifts in her seat. She cranes her neck. She squints.
She carries on, flying blind.

1:00 a.m. The friendly night becomes a graph of fear:
a jagged line between where-I-am and not-quite-sure.

The altimeter needle swirls wildly. It is broken!
(She will never know how high she is.)

She tries to outclimb the raging storm.
Up and up into the cold, brittle air.

The Vega struggles. It grows sluggish.
There is ice on the wings!

The plane reels under the ice's weight, pitching sideways.
Suddenly it spins, dipping and dizzying.

Everything she has ever learned courses through her blood.
Now or never. All or nothing.

She tenses up as the plane nose-dives downward.
She must accelerate to gain control.

How close is the water's surface? She bursts through the lowest clouds.
There it is, rushing toward her. Near. Nearer.

The Atlantic stares up with its huge uncaring eye.
Breakers rise like teeth from its angry mouth.

She hauls backward with all her strength. The Vega lurches.
It levels out—ten feet above the ocean tomb!

It is 3:00 a.m. Hour of drowse and snap-awake.
Hour of white knuckles.

Hour of flame streaming out of the cracked exhaust pipe.
Hour of being tested by the dark gods.

Hour of clammy gray. Hour of maybe—and maybe not.
Hour of *no* in the gut.

Alone, alone, alone, alone, alone.
Amelia Earhart sniffs salts. Sips juice from a can. Counts out loud.

Finds a middle between over and under.
Plunges once more into the thickness—and plows ahead.

6:00 a.m. How slowly the morning comes!
Black thins to a watery silt. The gloomy sky pales.

Splinters of sunlight stab down through cloud slits
and brace themselves on the vault of the open sea.

Amelia Earhart's eyes burn.
Her face is clenched like a stone mask.

Her stomach churns from the smell of leaking gas.
(A gauge above and behind her is dripping, drop after drop.)

She lowers the Vega through billowy snowfields.
Clouds are dragon heads, grinning monsters, floating dead fish.

On and on. On and on.
Anything but this endlessness of water!

Ah—there! A small boat! A drifting gull!
A coastline emerges, festered with boulders and crags.

Beyond it a mountain looms like a frightening wall.
Amelia Earhart veers north, following a line of train tracks.

An unseen clock is ticking. She must hurry,
racing a time bomb of exhaust flames and rising fumes.

The countryside spreads out like a green fan beneath her.
It is Ireland.

Past where the train tracks end, she spies a smooth pasture.
It must be here, she thinks. There is no other choice.

She circles between two fences. Cows startle and scatter.
The Vega descends, grazing the earth.

It lands with a jolt. It bumps slightly,
and rolls and rolls to a gradual stop.

Amelia Earhart leans back in the cockpit.
There is an unbelievable stillness inside her.

She slides open the window and blinks.
She lets out a deep breath.

Two thousand and twenty-six miles. Fourteen
hours and fifty-six minutes.
Alone.

A great peace wells up.
She knows she has crossed something more
than an ocean.

The world returns to her deafened ears. To be alive!
Insects. Bird calls. The rustle of uncut grass.

A farmer comes running, stiff-legged.
He stands gaping: a flying machine—with a woman inside it!

Amelia Earhart looks down. She pauses.
There is so much that one could say. But not now.

Instead, she smiles the widest smile of her entire life.
"Hi," she says simply. "Hi, I've come from America."

AFTERWORD

AMELIA EARHART is one of the most famous aviators in the history of flight. Born in 1897, in Atchison, Kansas, young Amelia was fun-loving and daring in her choice of childhood games, often sledding down high hills or even inventing her own homemade roller coaster! But that was only the beginning.

Serving as a nurse during World War I (1914-1918), Amelia was excited by the airplanes she observed in military training exercises. Soon she took her first airplane ride and shortly there-after purchased her own plane and took to the air.

During the 1920s she set many aviation records for speed, altitude, distance, and solo flights. She also lectured, wrote books and articles, and spoke up vigorously for a woman's right to equality in all areas of life.

In 1928 Amelia became the first woman to cross the Atlantic Ocean in an airplane, but on that trip she was only a passenger. Still, it led to her becoming an instant celebrity.

Her own *solo* flight across the Atlantic took place four years later. She was only the second person to do so—and the first woman. That flight, in a Lockheed Vega she nicknamed her *Little Red Bus*, went from Newfoundland, Canada, to its landing in Northern Ireland.

The flight departed on May 20, 1932, exactly five years to the day after the first transatlantic flight by Charles Lindbergh, and took roughly fifteen hours. The flight's difficulty and Amelia's courage increased her fame even more.

Her tragic last flight in 1937 was a failed attempt to fly around the world at the equator. Although she almost reached her final destination, her plane apparently ran out of gas and crashed into the Pacific Ocean.

The details of her crash—exactly when, where, and why—are still being debated. But what is clear is that Amelia Earhart will remain an American heroine for a long time.

TECHNICAL NOTE

Amelia Earhart sold her *Little Red Bus* Lockheed Vega to the Franklin Institute in Philadelphia in June 1933. Before turning the plane over to the institute, Amelia removed the engine, replacing it with a similar one, except for one detail: The replacement engine used a different exhaust system. Her Vega was gifted to the National Air and Space Museum in 1967, and currently displays that replacement engine and exhaust. The reader will note that the endpaper design in this book indicates the two different exhausts. The darker straight pipe represents the original design used during her historic transatlantic flight in 1932. The replacement exhaust running parallel to the fuselage is indicated in a lighter tone. I represented the replacement version in my paintings since this one is most familiar to museum visitors. —W. M.

BIBLIOGRAPHY

Backus, Jean L. *Letters from Amelia: An Intimate Portrait of Amelia Earhart.* Boston: Beacon Press, 1982.

Burke, John. *Winged Legend.* New York: G. P. Putnam's Sons, 1970.

Earhart, Amelia. *The Fun of It.* Chicago: Academy Press Limited, 1977.

Lovell, Mary S. *The Sound of Wings: The Life of Amelia Earhart.* New York: St. Martin's Press, 1989.

Rich, Doris L. *Amelia Earhart: A Biography.* Washington and London: Smithsonian Institution Press, 1989.

Van Pelt, Lori. *Amelia Earhart: The Sky's No Limit.* New York: Tom Doherty Associates, LLL, 2005.

INTERNET RESOURCES

THERE IS ALSO A GREAT DEAL OF MATERIAL RELATING TO AMELIA EARHART'S LIFE AND ACHIEVEMENTS ON THE INTERNET. A FEW OF THESE SOURCES ARE LISTED BELOW FOR FURTHER READING.

The official website of Amelia Earhart is www.ameliaearhart.com.

You can find a biography of Amelia Earhart, as well as facts and pictures, at www.acepilots.com/earhart.html.

Smithsonian National Air and Space Museum: www.nasm.si.edu

George Palmer Putnam Collection: www.lib.purdue.edu/spcol/aearhart

THINGS AMELIA SAID

IN HER TALKS, BOOKS, AND ARTICLES, AMELIA EARHART SAID MANY THINGS ABOUT AVIATION, A WOMAN'S PLACE IN THE WORLD, AND THE IMPORTANCE OF COURAGE. HERE ARE A FEW OF THEM.

"The most effective way to do it, is to do it."

"You can do anything you decide to do. You can act to change and control your life, and the procedure, the process, is its own reward."

"One of my favorite phobias is that girls, especially those whose tastes aren't routine, often don't get a fair break. . . . It has come down through the generations, an inheritance of age-old customs which produced the corollary that women are bred to timidity."

"Everyone has his own Atlantics to fly. Whatever you want very much to do, against the opposition of tradition, neighborhood opinion, and so-called common sense—that is an Atlantic."

"The lure of flying is the lure of beauty."

"I could not see. I carried on."

"Please know I am aware of the hazards. I want to do it because I want to do it. Women must try to do things as men have tried."

"Spring hints its coming first for birds and aviators."

"The actual doing of a dangerous thing may require little courage. The preparation for it—the acceptance of the inevitable risks involved—may be a far greater test of morale."

"I prefer good mechanical work to rabbits' feet."

"Courage is the price that life exacts for granting peace."

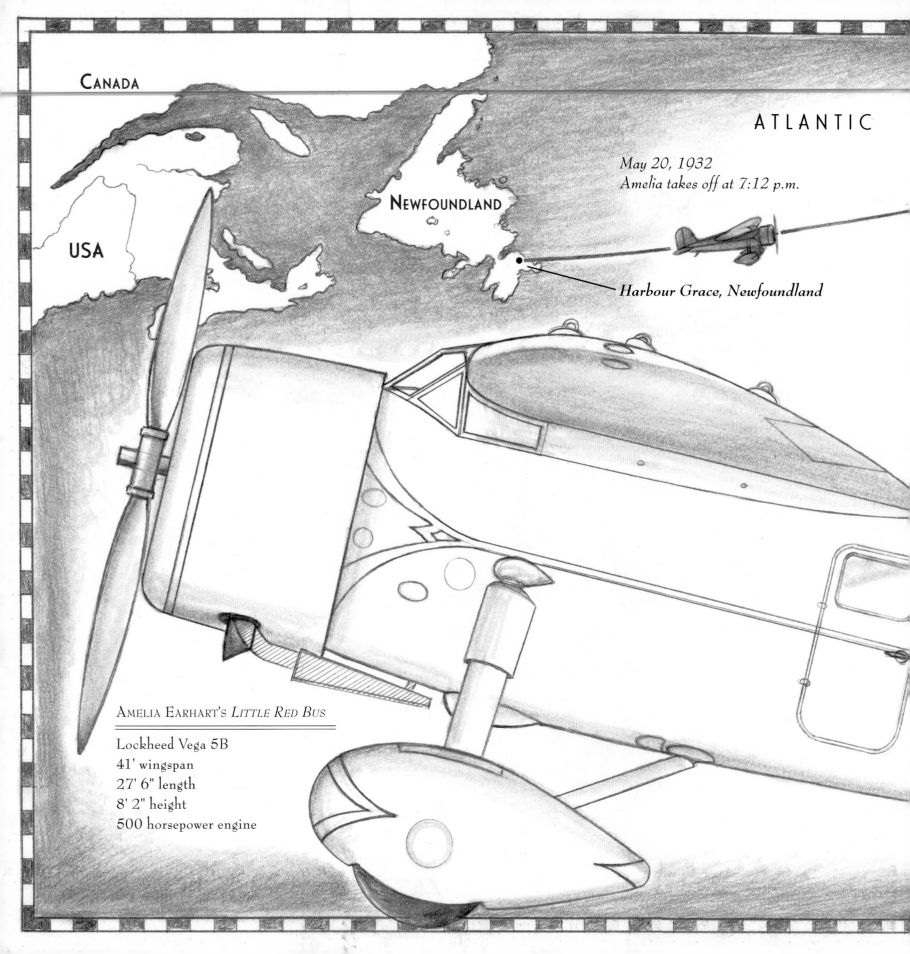

CANADA

ATLANTIC

May 20, 1932
Amelia takes off at 7:12 p.m.

NEWFOUNDLAND

USA

Harbour Grace, Newfoundland

AMELIA EARHART'S *LITTLE RED BUS*

Lockheed Vega 5B
41' wingspan
27' 6" length
8' 2" height
500 horsepower engine